Langenscheidt

Italian
at your Fingertips

Tien Tammada

Langenscheidt

Foreword

Traveling to foreign or to distant lands is a wonderful and exciting thing to do. In fact, it probably features top of the list in worldwide rankings.

However, before every journey to a foreign country, there is a hurdle to be cleared and this hurdle is called "foreign languages". For many, this hurdle seems insurmountable. As a result, they have to give up their life's dream.

What a pity!

You may be planning a week's holiday in Italy to experience the magical countryside or considering moving to live and work in an Italian-speaking country. You might want to flirt or just understand when someone is trying to flirt with you (after all, you don't want to miss the chance to meet the prince or princess of your dreams, do you?).

Whatever your motivation, don't wait.
Don't let this hurdle stop you from fulfilling your lifelong dreams!
Take courage to embark on this exciting journey to the Italian language

-now!

Once you've made the decision, you'll find that this book provides you with the first helpful steps. You don't need to book a language course and you don't need to worry about complicated grammatical points.

Anyone who has learnt to master a foreign language knows that the essential and really crucial thing about learning a language is actually quite simple: you need to jump in at the deep end. Once you're in the water, everything flows from there.

Jump and don't think twice! You'll learn by doing, not by preparing. The pictures, the selection of important words and useful phrases that you'll find in this book are an important first step. As soon as you come up against the first language hurdle, you can open the book at the appropriate page and find the necessary words and phrases.

If that doesn't work, try pointing to the relevant picture or sentence with your finger. People will know immediately what you mean.
It's really all very easy and convenient. That's why the book is called:

"Italian at your Fingertips".

Content

Useful daily conversations

Nella quotidianita [nella kuotidijani'ta]

Greeting

Saluto [sa'lu:to]

Buongiorno !	Buonasera !	Ciao !
[buon'dʒorno]	[buona'se:ra]	['tʃa:o]
Good morning!	Good evening!	Hello!

Come va?

['ko:me va]

How are you?

Bene, grazie.

['bɛ:ne, 'grattsje]

I'm fine, thank you.

Sì. | No.

[si] | [nɔ]

Yes. | No.

Grazie.	Grazie mille.	Di niente.	Con piacere.
['grattsje]	['grattsje 'mille]	[di 'njɛnte]	[kon pja'tʃe:re]
Thanks.	Thank you very much.	You're welcome.	With pleasure.

Mi chiamo… [mi 'kja:mo]	My name is …
Come si chiama? ['ko:me si 'kja:ma]	What is your name? (formal)
Come ti chiami? ['ko:me ti 'kja:mi]	What is your name? (informal)
Piacere. [pja'tʃe:re]	Nice to meet you.
Vengo dagli Stati Uniti. ['vɛngo 'daʎʎi 'sta:ti u'niti]	I'm from the United States.
Non parlo italiano. [non 'parlo ita'lja:no]	I don't speak Italian.
Parlo italiano, ma solo un po'. ['parlo ita'lja:no, ma 'so:lo 'un pɔ]	I speak a little Italian.
Potrebbe parlare più lentamente, per favore? [pɔt'reb'bɛ par'la:re pju lenta'mente per fa'vo:re]	Could you speak a little more slowly, please?
Come si dice in italiano? ['ko:me si 'di:tʃe in ita'lja:no]	How do you say that in Italian?

Cosa significa?	What does that mean?
['kɔ:sa siɲ'ɲi:fika]	
Che cosa è? / Cos'è?	What is that?
[ke 'kɔ:sa ɛ / kɔ'sɛ]	
Come sta?	How are you? (formal)
['ko:me 'sta]	
Come stai?	How are you? (informal)
['ko:me 'stai]	
Bene, grazie. E Lei / tu?	Fine , thank you.
['bɛ:ne, 'grattsje e 'lɛ:i /tu]	And you? (formal / informal)
Capisco.	I understand.
[ka'pisko]	
Scusi, non ho capito.	Sorry, I didn't understand.
['sku:zi non ɔ ka'pi:to]	
Come dice?	Pardon?
['ko:me 'di:tʃe]	
Scusi!	Excuse me! / Sorry!
['sku:zi]	
Nessun problema.	No problem.
[nes'sun pro'blɛ:ma]	
Non c'è problema.	No problem.
[non 'tʃɛ pro'blɛ:ma]	
Mi può aiutare, per favore?	Could you help me, please?
[mi 'puɔ aju'ta:re per fa'vo:re]	

Dov'è...? [do'vɛ]	Where is...?
Vorrei... [vor'rɛːi]	I would like...
C'è... / Ci sono...? [tʃɛ.../ tʃi 'soːno]	Is there...? / Are there...?
Quanto costa...? ['kuanto 'kɔsta]	How much does it cost...?
D'accordo! [dak'kɔrdo]	Agree!
bene ['bɛːne]	good
molto bene ['molto 'bɛːne]	very good
Mi piace. [mi 'pjaːtʃe]	I like this.
Non mi piace. [non mi 'pjaːtʃe]	I don't like that.
Così così [ko'si ko'si]	So-so.
Va bene! [va 'bɛːne]	All right!
Certo! ['tʃɛrto]	Sure!/ Certain! / Of course!

Ottimo! ['ɔttimo]	Great!
Eccellente! [ettʃel'lɛnte]	Excellent!
Meraviglioso! [meraviʎ'ʎo:so]	Marvelous!
male ['ma:le]	bad
tanto ['tanto]	a lot
un po'. ['un pɔ]	a little
Un momento, per favore. [un mo'mento per fa'vo:re]	One moment, please.
Un attimo, per favore. [un 'attimo per fa'vo:re]	Just a moment, please.
A presto! [a 'prɛsto]	See you soon!
A dopo! / A più tardi! [a 'do:po / a pju 'tardi]	See you later!
A domani! [a do'ma:ni]	See you tomorrow!

Arrivederci! [arrive'dertʃı]	Good bye! / See you again!
Ciao! ['tʃa:o]	Bye!
Chi? [ki]	Who?
Cosa? ['kɔ:sa]	What?
Dove? ['do:ve]	Where?
Dov'è...? [do'vɛ]	Where is...?
Dove sono...? ['do:ve 'so:no]	Where are...?
Quando? ['kuando]	When?
Perché? [per'ke]	Why?
Come? ['ko:me]	How?
Quanto? ['kuanto]	How much? / How many?

l'aeroporto
[laero'pɔrto]

the airport

Dov'è il controllo dei passaporti?
[do'vɛ il kon'trɔllo dei passa'pɔrti]

Where is the passport control?

L'AEREO [la'ɛːreõ]

Scusi, come si arriva in centro?
['skuːzi 'koːme si ar'riːva in 'tʃɛntro]
Excuse me, how can I get to the city center?

Dov'è la stazione?
[do'vɛ la stat'tsjoːne]
Where is the train station?

[uʃˈʃita] **Exit**

Mi scusi, dov'è l'uscita?

[mi ˈskuːzi doˈvɛ luʃˈʃiːta]

Excuse me, where is the exit?

the airplane

Dov'è la fermata dell'autobus?

[doˈvɛ la ferˈmaːta delˈlaːutobus]

Where is the bus stop?

Dove posso prendere un taxi?

[ˈdoːve ˈposso ˈprɛndere un ˈtaksi]

Where can I get a taxi?

Dov'è l'ufficio turistico?
[do'vɛ luf'fi:tʃo tu'ristiko]
Where is tourist information?

Quanto è lontano il centro città?
['kuanto ɛ lon'ta:no il 'tʃɛntro tʃit'ta]
How far is it to the city center?

Conosce un hotel economico?
[ko'noʃʃe un o'tɛl eko'nɔ:miko]
Do you know an inexpensive hotel?

Per favore, mi porti a questo indirizzo.
[per fa'vo:re mi 'porti a 'kuesto indi'rittso]
Would you please drive me to this address?

il taxi
[il 'taksi]

taxi

Quanto costa il viaggio?

['kuanto 'kɔsta il vi'addʒo]

How much does the ride cost?

Posso pagare con carta di credito?

['posso pa'ga:re kon 'karta di 'kre:dito]

Can I pay by credit card?

Può dirmi quando devo scendere, per favore?

['pu·ɔ 'dirmi 'kuando 'dɛ:vo 'ʃendere per fa'vo:re]

Could you tell me when to get off please?

Grazie per il Suo aiuto.

['grattsje per il 'su:o a'ju:to]

Thank you very much for your help.

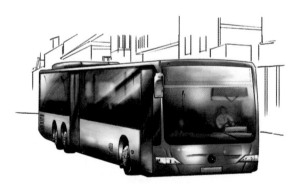

il bus / l'autobus
[il bus / 'la:utobus]
bus

il treno
[il trɛ:no]

---

train

la metropolitana
[la metropoli'ta:na]

---

underground

il tram
[il tram]

---

tram

il TAV (Treno Alta Velocità)

[il 'tav]   ['trɛːno 'alta velotʃi'ta]

HST (High Speed Train)

la nave

[la 'naːve]

ship

Accommodation

L'alloggio [lal'lɔddʒo]

Avete delle camere disponibili?
[a've:te 'delle 'ka:mere dispo'ni:bili]

Is there any room available?

Posso vedere la camera?
['pɔsso ve'de:re la 'ka:mera]

May I see the room, please?

Quanto costa?
['kuanto 'kɔsta]

How much is it?

La colazione è inclusa?
[la kolat'tsjo:ne ɛ in'klu:za]

Is breakfast included?

Ho prenotato una camera
a nome di ...
[ɔ preno'ta:to una 'ka:mera
a 'no:me di]

I have booked a room in
the name of...

Ecco il mio passaporto.
['ɛkko il 'mi:o passa'pɔrto]

Here is my passport.

Avete il Wi-Fi?
[aˈvːte il ˈwiːfi]

Do you have Wi-Fi?

C'è una cassaforte?
[tʃɛ ˈuːna kassaˈfɔrte]

Do you have a safe?

Quando devo lasciare la stanza?
[ˈkuando ˈdɛːvo la ʃ ˈʃaːre la ˈstantsa]

When do I have to check out?

C'è sempre qualcuno alla reception?
[ˈtʃɛ ˈsɛmpre kualˈkuːno alla reˈsɛpʃon]

Is reception open all the time?

C'è un ristorante nell'hotel?
[ˈtʃɛ un ristoˈrante nelloˈtɛl]

Is there a restaurant in this hotel?

Vorrei una camera per...

[vor'rɛ:i una 'ka:mera per]

I would like a room for…

una persona.

['u:na per'sona]

one (person).

due persone.

['du:e per'so:ne]

two (people).

una famiglia.
[ˈuːna faˈmiʎʎa]

a family.

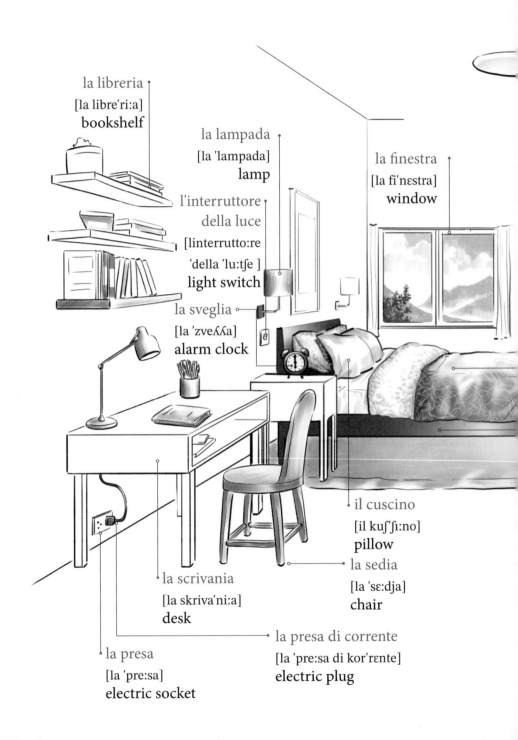

la libreria
[la libre'ri:a]
bookshelf

la lampada
[la 'lampada]
lamp

la finestra
[la fi'nɛstra]
window

l'interruttore
della luce
[linterrutto:re
'della 'lu:tʃe]
light switch

la sveglia
[la 'zveʎʎa]
alarm clock

il cuscino
[il kuʃ'ʃi:no]
pillow

la scrivania
[la skriva'ni:a]
desk

la sedia
[la 'sɛ:dja]
chair

la presa di corrente
[la 'pre:sa di kor'rɛnte]
electric plug

la presa
[la 'pre:sa]
electric socket

l'aria condizionata
['la:rja kondittsjo'na:ta]
air conditioner

la tenda
[la 'tɛnda]
curtain

l'appendiabiti
[lappɛndi'a:biti]
clothes hanger

la camicia
[la ka'mi:tʃa]
shirt

il cappello
[il kap'pɛllo]
hat

a cassettiera
kasset'tjɛ:ra]
drawer

la borsetta
[la bor'setta]
handbag

la maglietta
[la maʎ'ʎetta]
T-shirt

i pantaloni
[i panta'lo:ni]
pants

le scarpe
[le 'skarpe]
shoes

la coperta
[la ko'pɛrta]
blanket

il letto
[il 'lɛtto]
bed

il tappeto
[il tap'pe:to]
carpet

In the bedroom

Nella camera da letto [nella 'ka:mera da 'lɛtto]

In the bathroom

Nel bagno [nel 'baɲɲo]

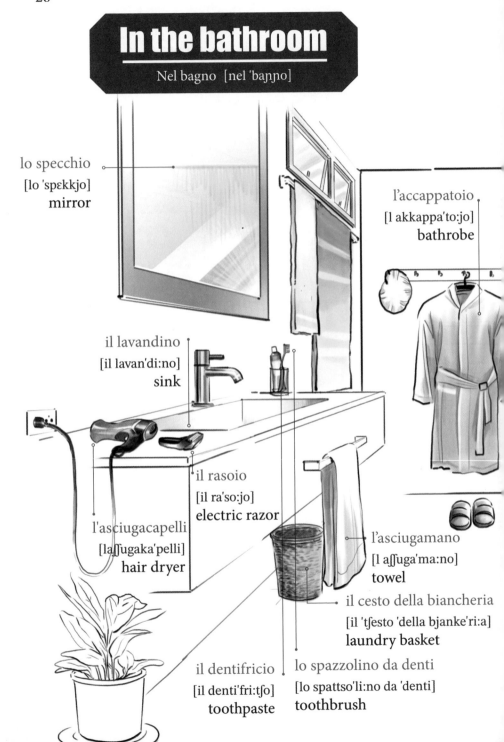

lo specchio
[lo 'spɛkkjo]
mirror

l'accappatoio
[l akkappa'to:jo]
bathrobe

il lavandino
[il lavan'di:no]
sink

il rasoio
[il ra'so:jo]
electric razor

l'asciugacapelli
[laʃʃugaka'pelli]
hair dryer

l'asciugamano
[l aʃʃuga'ma:no]
towel

il cesto della biancheria
[il 'tʃesto 'della bjanke'ri:a]
laundry basket

il dentifricio
[il denti'fri:tʃo]
toothpaste

lo spazzolino da denti
[lo spattso'li:no da 'denti]
toothbrush

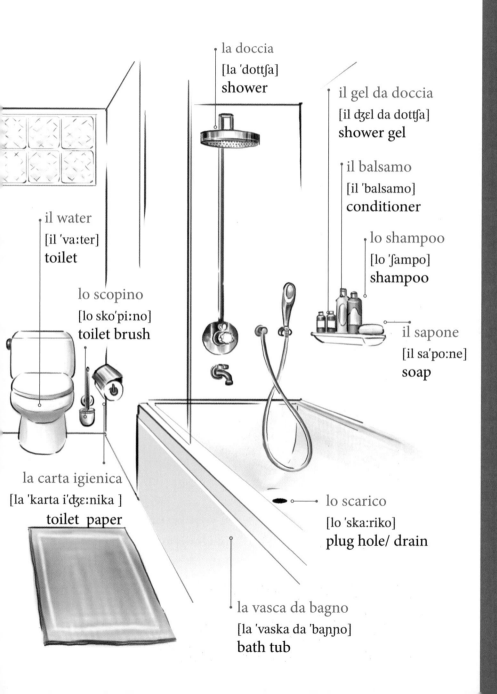

la doccia
[la 'dottʃa]
shower

il gel da doccia
[il dʒɛl da dottʃa]
shower gel

il balsamo
[il 'balsamo]
conditioner

lo shampoo
[lo 'ʃampo]
shampoo

il water
[il 'vaːter]
toilet

lo scopino
[lo sko'piːno]
toilet brush

il sapone
[il sa'poːne]
soap

la carta igienica
[la 'karta i'dʒeːnika]
toilet paper

lo scarico
[lo 'skaːriko]
plug hole/ drain

la vasca da bagno
[la 'vaska da 'baɲɲo]
bath tub

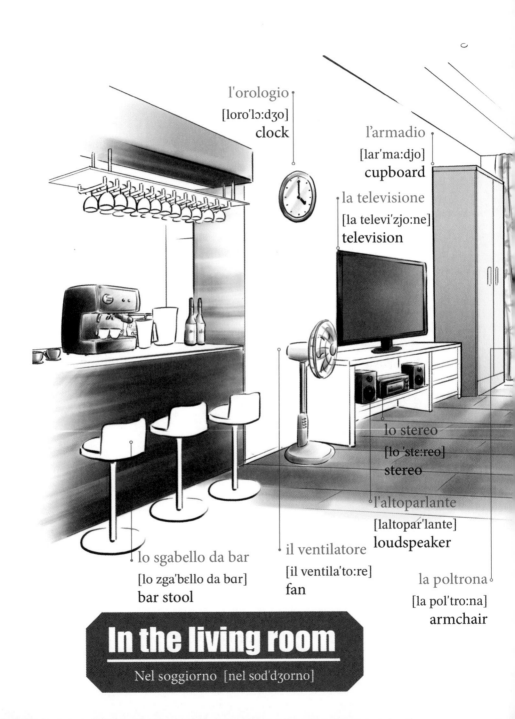

l'orologio
[loro'lɔ:dʒo]
clock

l'armadio
[lar'ma:djo]
cupboard

la televisione
[la televi'zjo:ne]
television

lo stereo
[lo 'stɛ:reo]
stereo

l'altoparlante
[laltopar'lante]
loudspeaker

lo sgabello da bar
[lo zga'bɛllo da bɑr]
bar stool

il ventilatore
[il ventila'to:re]
fan

la poltrona
[la pol'tro:na]
armchair

In the living room

Nel soggiorno [nel sod'dʒorno]

il pianoforte
[il pjano'fɔrte]
piano

il quadro
[il 'kua:dro]
picture

i libri
[i 'li:bri]
books

il violino
[il vjo'li:no]
violin

il vaso
[il 'va:zo]
vase

il divano
[il di'va:no]
sofa

il telefono
[il te'lɛ:fono]
telephone

i fiori
[i 'fjo:ri]
flowers

il telecomando
[il teleko'mando]
remote control

la tazza
[la 'tattsa]
cup

la padella
[la pa'dɛlla]
frying pan

il calice
[il 'kalitʃe]
wine glass

la bottiglia
[la bot'tiʎʎa]
bottle

il piatto
[il 'pjatto]
plate

il cucchiaio
[il kuk'kja:jo]
spoon

la forchetta
[la for'ketta]
fork

il rubinetto
[il rubi'netto]
faucet

il forno a microonde
[il 'forno a mikro'onde]
microwave

il tagliere
[il taʎ'ʎɛːre]
chopping board

In the kitchen

nella cucina   [nella ku'tʃiːna]

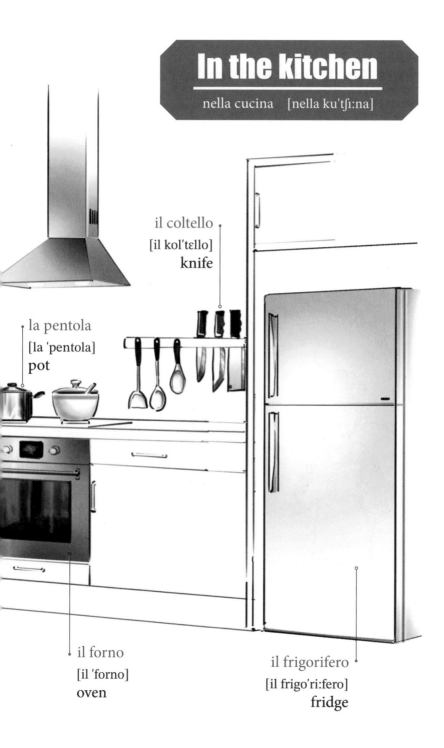

il coltello
[il kol'tɛllo]
knife

la pentola
[la 'pentola]
pot

il forno
[il 'forno]
oven

il frigorifero
[il frigo'riːfero]
fridge

Excursions (In the city and in the countryside)

Escursioni (in città e fuori città) [eskur'sjo:ni in tʃit'ta o fu'ɔ:ri tʃit'ta]

Cosa c'è d'interessante da queste parti?

['kɔ:sa 'tʃɛ dinteres'sante da 'kueste 'parti]

Are there any tourist attractions in this area?

Dove posso gustare dei piatti locali?

['doːve 'posso gus'taːre 'deːi pjat'ti lo'kaːli]

Where can I taste the traditional local food?

Excursions by train

Viaggi in treno ['vjaddʒi in 'trɛːno]

Dov'è la stazione ferroviaria?
[do'vɛ la stat'tsjoːne ferro'vjaːrja]

Where is the train station?

Dov'è la biglietteria?
[do'vɛ la biʎʎette'riːa]

Where is the ticket office?

Quanto costa il biglietto?
['kuanto 'kɔsta il biʎ'ʎetto]

How much does the ticket cost?

Un biglietto di prima classe, per favore.
[un biʎ'ʎetto di 'priːma 'klasse per fa'voːre]

One first-class ticket, please.

Un biglietto di seconda classe, per favore.
[un biʎ'ʎetto di se'konda 'klasse per fa'voːre]

One second-class ticket, please.

Un biglietto di sola andata, per favore.
[un biʎ'ʎetto di 'soːla an'data per fa'voːre]

A one-way ticket, please.

Un biglietto di andata e ritorno, per favore.
[un biʎ'ʎetto di an'daːta e ri'torno per fa'voːre]

A return ticket, please.

Vorrei prenotare un posto.
[vor'rɛ:i preno'ta:re un 'posto]

I would like to reserve a seat, please.

Quando parte il treno?
['kuando 'parte il 'trɛ:no]

What time does the train leave?

Quante volte devo cambiare treno?
['kuante 'volte 'dɛ:vo kam'bja:re 'trɛ:no]

How many times do I have to change trains?

Qual è la prossima stazione?
[kua'lɛ la 'prossima stat'tsjo:ne]

What is the next station called?

Per favore, mi dica quando
devo scendere.
[per fa'vo:re mi 'di:ka 'kuando
'dɛ:vo 'ʃendere]

Would you please tell me when I have to get off?

At the train station

Alla stazione ferroviaria

[alla sta'tsjo:ne ferro'vja:rja]

la stazione
[la stat'tsjo:ne]
station

la stazione centrale
[la stat'tsjo:ne t∫en'tra:le]
central station

la biglietteria
[la biʎʎette'ri:a]
ticket office

il biglietto
[il biʎ'ʎetto]
ticket

l'orario
[lo'ra:rjo]
timetable

l'arrivo
[lar'riv:o]
arrival

la partenza
[la par'tɛntsa]
departure

il treno
[il 'trɛ:no]
train

la piattaforma
[la pjatta'forma]
platform

il vagone letto
[il va'go:ne 'letto]
sleeping carriage

l'espresso
[les'prɛsso]
express train

un biglietto di prima classe
[un biʎ'ʎetto di 'pri:ma 'klasse]
a first-class ticket

un biglietto di seconda classe
[un biʎ'ʎet to di se'konda 'klasse]
a second-class ticket

la prenotazione del posto
[la prenotat'tsjo:ne del 'posto]
seat reservation

andata
[an'da:ta]
one-way

andata e ritorno
[an'da:ta e ri'torno]
return

il supplemento
[il supple'mento]
surcharge

salire
[sa'li:re]
board

scendere
['ʃendere]
get off

cambiare il treno
[kam'bja:re il'trɛ:no]
change trains

Quando parte il treno / l'autobus / la metropolitana / il tram?

['kuando 'parte il 'trɛːno / 'laːutobus /
la metropoli'taːna / il tram]

What time does the train / the bus
the underground / the tram leave?

Mi scusi, mi aiuterebbe ad acquistare un biglietto all'automatico?

[mi 'sku:zi mi ajute'rɛbbe ad akkui'sta:re
un biʎ'ʎetto allauto'ma:tiko]

Excuse me, can you help me to buy
a ticket from the machine?

Voglio andare a...

[voʎ'ʎo an'da:re a]

I want to go to…

Excursions by bus and tram

Escursioni in autobus e con il tram

[eskur'sjo:ni in 'a:utobus e kon il tram]

---

l'autobus / il bus

['la:utobus / il bus]

bus

---

la fermata del bus

[la fer'ma:ta del bus]

bus stop

---

il tram

[il tram]

tram

Dov'è la fermata del tram?

[do'vɛ la fer'ma:ta del tram]

Where is the tram stop?

---

la fermata del tram

[la fer'ma:ta del tram]

tram stop

---

il biglietto

[il biʎ'ʎetto]

ticket

---

il controllore

[il kontrol'lo:re]

ticket inspector

---

la multa

[la 'multa]

fine/penalty

DOV' È...?

[doˈvɛ]

Where is…?

Dov'è la fermata dell'autobus?

[doˈvɛ la ferˈmaːta delˈlaːutobus]

Where is the bus stop?

il semaforo
[il se'ma:foro]
traffic lights

la moto / la motocicletta
[la 'mɔːto / la mototʃi'kletta]
motorcycle

la bicicletta
[la bitʃi'kletta]
bicycle

la macchina / l'automobile
[la 'makkina / l'auto'mɔːbile]
car

Traveling on your own by car, motocycle, bicycle and on foot

Viaggiare da soli in auto, in moto, in bicicletta e a piedi
[viad'dʒa:re da 'so:li in 'a:uto in 'mɔ:to in bitʃi'kletta e a 'pje:di]

la strada [la 'stra:da]	street
l'incrocio ['linkro:tʃo]	intersection
il passaggio pedonale [il pas'saddʒo pedo'na:le]	pedestrian crossing
andare dritto [an'da:re 'dritto]	go straight on
a destra [a 'dɛstra]	to the right
a sinistra [a si'nistra]	to the left
qui /qua [kui/kua]	here / there
là [la]	over there
vicino [vi'tʃi:no]	near
lontano [lon'ta:no]	far
Dov'è una stazione di servizio? [do'vɛ 'u:na stat'tsjo:ne di ser'vittsjo]	Where is a petrol station?

Art and leisure time activities

Arte ed attività di svago ['arte edattivi'ta di 'zva:go]

---

il teatro

[il te'a:tro]
the theater

---

il teatro dell'opera

[il te'a:tro dell 'ɔ:pera]
the opera house

---

il cinema

[il 'tʃi:nema]
the cinema

---

la galleria d'arte

[la galle'ri:a 'darte]
the art gallery

---

il museo

[il mu'zɛ:o]
the museum

la piscina coperta
[la piʃˈʃiːna koˈpɛrta]
the indoor swimming pool

la piscina scoperta
[la piʃˈʃiːna skoˈpɛrta]
the outdoor swimming pool

la sauna
[la ˈsaːuna]
the sauna

il parco comunale
[il ˈparko komuˈnaːle]
the city park

la palestra
[la paˈlɛstra]
the gym

Tourist attractions

Attrazioni turistiche [attrat'tsjo:ni tu'ristike]

I Fori Imperiali
the Imperial Fora

Il Colosseo
the Colosseum

Piazza di Spagna
Square of Spain

Piazza Navona
Square Navona

Castel Sant'Angelo
Sant'Angelo Castel

Fontana di Trevi
the Trevi Fountain

Trastevere
Trastevere

Vaticano
Vatican City

Tourist attractions

Attrazioni turistiche [attrat'tsjo:ni tu'ristike]

La Valle dei Templi (Agrigento)
Valley of the Temples

I Trulli (Alberobello)
the Trulli of Alberobello

Il Duomo (Milano)
Duomo Milano Cathedral

Napoli e il Vesuvio
Naples and mount Vesuvius

La Torre di Pisa
Leaning Tower of Pisa

Ponte Vecchio (Firenze)
the Ponte Vicchio in Florence

San Gimignano (Toscana)
San Gimignano in Tuscany

At the bakery

Panificio [paniˈfiːtʃo]

lo sfilatino
[lo sfilaˈtiːno]

baguette

la michetta
[la miˈketta]

michetta

il cornetto
[il korˈnetto]

croissant

il pancarrè
[il pankarˈre]

plain loaf

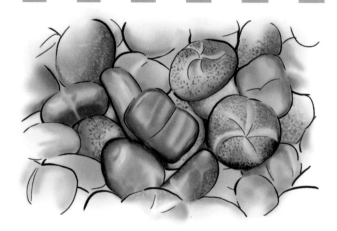

il panino
[il pa'ni:no]

---

bread roll

il pane ai cereali
[il 'pa:ne 'a:i tʃere'a:li]

---

cereal bread

il pane casereccio
[il 'pa:ne kase'rettʃo]

---

homemade bread

la pecora
[la 'pɛːkora]
lamb

la carne di pecora
[la 'karne di 'pɛːkora]
sheep meat / mutton

il coniglio
[il ko'niʎʎo]
rabbit

l'anatra
['laːnatra]
duck

la mucca
[la 'mukka]
cow

il manzo
[il 'mandzo]
beef

At the butchers

In macelleria [in matʃelle'riːa]

il maiale
[il ma'jaːle]
pork

il salame
[il sa'laːme]
salami sausage

la carne
[la 'karne]
meat

il pollo
[il 'pollo]
chicken

At the fishmonger

In pescheria [in peske'ri:a]

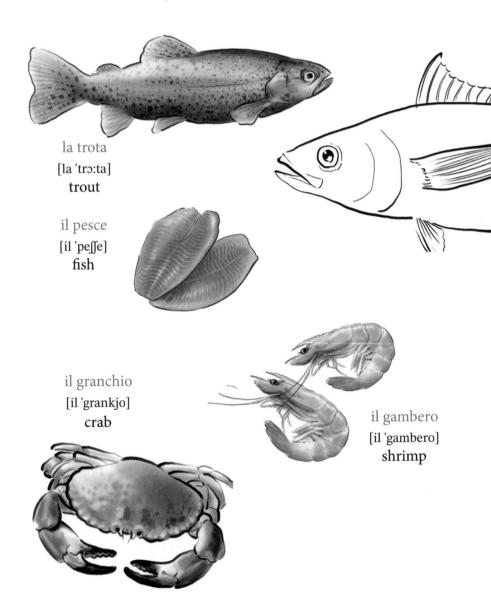

la trota
[la 'trɔ:ta]
trout

il pesce
[il 'peʃʃe]
fish

il granchio
[il 'grankjo]
crab

il gambero
[il 'gambero]
shrimp

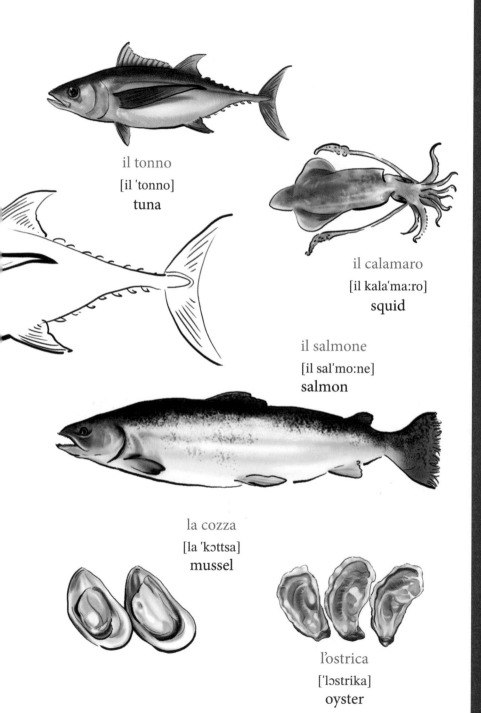

il tonno
[il 'tonno]
tuna

il calamaro
[il kala'ma:ro]
squid

il salmone
[il sal'mo:ne]
salmon

la cozza
[la 'kɔttsa]
mussel

l'ostrica
['lɔstrika]
oyster

1

2

3

4

5

6

7

8

9

In the vegetable shop

Dall'erbivendolo [dallerbi'vendolo]

---

1. la melanzana
[la melan'dza:na] aubergine

2. il cetriolo
[il tʃetri'ɔ:lo] cucumber

3. i broccoli
[i 'brɔkkoli] broccoli

4. il carciofo
[il kar'tʃɔ:fo] artichoke

5. il radicchio
[il ra'dikkjo] radiccho

6. i piselli
[i pi'sɛlli] peas

7. il cavolfiore
[il kavol'fjo:re] cauliflower

8. la carota
[la ka'rɔ:ta] carrot

9. il basilico
[il ba'zi:liko] basil

1. lo zenzero
[lo 'dzendzero] ginger

2. la lattuga
[la lat'tu:ga] lettuce

3. la zucca
[la 'tsukka] pumpkin

4. la mandorla
[la 'mandorla] almond

5. l'arachide
[la'ra:kide] peanut

6. la nocciola
[la not'tʃɔ:la] hazelnut

7. l'aglio
['laʎʎo] garlic

8. il fungo
[il 'fungo] mushroom

9. la patata
[la pa'ta:ta] potato

10. il mais
[il 'mais] corn

11. la noce
[la 'no:tʃe] walnut

1

2

3

4

5

6

7

8

9

10

1. la barbabietola
[la barba'bjɛ:tola] beetroot

———

2. il peperone
[il pepe'ro:ne] sweet pepper

———

3. la cipolla
[la tʃi'polla] onion

———

4. il cavolo bianco
[il 'ka:volo 'bjanko] white cabbage

———

5. il cavolo rosso
[il 'ka:volo 'rosso] red cabbage

———

6. gli asparagi
[ʎi as'pa:radʒi] asparagus

———

7. il pomodoro
[il pomo'dɔ:ro] tomato

———

8. la zucchina
[la tsuk'ki:na] courgette

———

9. il sedano
[il 'sɛ:dano] celery

———

10. gli spinaci
[ʎi spi'na:tʃi] spinach

la mela	la mela verde	la pera
[la 'me:la]	[la 'me:la 'verde]	[la 'pe:ra]
apple	**green apple**	**pear**

la ciliegia	la prugna	l'oliva
[la tʃi'ljɛ:dʒa]	[la 'pruɲɲa]	[lo'li:va]
cherry	**plum**	**olive**

la noce di cocco	la fragola	l'ananas
[la 'no:tʃe di 'kɔkko]	[la 'fra:gola]	['lananas]
coconut	**strawberry**	**pineapple**

il melograno

[il melo'gra:no]

pomegranate

la mora

[la 'mɔ:ra]

blackberry

il lampone

[il lam'po:ne]

raspberry

In the fruit shop

Dal fruttivendolo [dal frutti'vendolo]

il mirtillo

[il mir'tillo]

blueberry

il ribes nero

[il 'ri:bes 'ne:ro]

blackcurrant

il ribes rosso

[il 'ri:bes 'rosso]

redcurrant

la limetta

[la li'metta]

lime

il limone

[il li'mo:ne]

lemon

l'avocado

[lavo'ka:do]

avocado

la pesca

[la 'pɛska]

peach

la papaia

[la pa'pa:ja]

papaya

la banana

[la ba'na:na]

banana

il mango

[il 'maŋgo]

mango

l'arancia
[la'rantʃa]
orange

il mandarino
[il manda'ri:no]
tangerine

l'anguria
[lan'gu:rja]
watermelon

l'uva
['lu:va]
grape

il melone
[il me'lo:ne]
melon

il kiwi
[il 'ki:wi]
kiwi

Beverages

Le bevande [le be'vande]

l'acqua

['lakkua]
still water

l'acqua gassata /
l'acqua frizzante

['lakkua gas'sa:ta /
'lakkua frid'dzante]
sparkling water

l'acqua minerale

['lakkua mine'ra:le]
mineral water

la limonata

[la limo'na:ta]
lemonade

le bibite

[le 'bi:bite]
soft drinks

il succo di carota
[il 'sukko di ka'rɔ:ta]
carrot juice

il succo d'ananas
[il 'sukko 'dananas]
pineapple juice

il succo di mela
[il 'sukko di 'me:la]
apple juice

il succo di pomodoro
[il 'sukko di pomo'dɔ:ro]
tomato juice

il succo d'arancia
[il 'sukko da'rantʃa]
orange juice

il succo d'uva
[il 'sukko 'du:va]
grape juice

At the bar

Al bar [al bar]

il prosecco
[il proˈsekko]
prosecco

la grappa
[la ˈgrappa]
grappa

il digestivo
[il didʒesˈtiːvo]
digestive

la birra
[la ˈbirra]
beer

il vino rosso
[il ˈviːno ˈrosso]
red wine

il vino bianco
[il ˈviːno ˈbjanko]
white wine

il vino rosé
[il ˈviːno roˈze]
rosé wine

Nel vino sta la verità. (latino: in vino veritas)
[nel ˈviːno sta la veriˈta] The truth is in the wine.

Il vino è poesia in bottiglia.
[il ˈviːno ɛ poeˈziːa in botˈtiʎʎa] Wine is poetry in a bottle.

Anche il vino bianco fa un naso rosso.
[ˈanke il ˈviːno ˈbjanko fa un ˈnaːso ˈrosso]
White wine can also make your nose red.

La vita
è troppo corta
per bere
vino
cattivo.

[la vita ɛ ˈtrɔppo ˈkorta per ˈbeːre ˈviːno katˈtiːvo]

Life is too short to drink bad wine.

Johann Wolfgang von Goethe

l'espresso
[les'prɛsso]

il macchiato
[il mak'kja:to]

il caffè lungo
[il kaf'fɛ 'lungo]

il caffè con panna
[il kaf'fɛ kon 'panna]

l'affogato
[laffo'ga:to]

At the coffee shop

Nel caffè [nel kaf'fɛ]

l'espresso
coffee with a very strong taste

il macchiato
double espresso with some milk froth

il caffè lungo
espresso diluted with water

il caffè con panna
espresso with [whipped] cream

l'affogato
vanilla ice cream in espresso

il caffelatte
[il kaffɛˈlatte]

il cappuccino
[il kapputˈtʃiːno]

il caffè corretto
[il kafˈfɛ korˈrɛtto]

la cioccolata calda
[la tʃokkoˈlaːta ˈkalda]

il latte caldo
[il ˈlatte ˈkaldo]

il caffelatte

milk coffee

il cappuccino

milk coffee with little milk froth

il caffè corretto

espresso with liqueur and milk froth

la cioccolata calda

hot chocolat

il latte caldo

hot milk

Tea

tè [te]

1. il tè nero
[il te 'ne:ro]
black tea

2. il tè bianco
[il te 'bjanko]
white tea

3. il tè verde
[il te 'verde]
green tea

4. il tè alla frutta
[il te 'alla 'frutta]
fruit tea

5. il tè giallo
[il te 'dʒallo]
yellow tea

6. la tisana
[la ti'zana]
herbal tea

Mi scusi, vorrei ordinare.

[mi 'sku:zi vor'rɛːi ordi'naːre]

Excuse me, I would like to order, please.

Qual è la specialità del posto?

['kuaːl ɛ la spetʃali'ta del 'posto]

What are the specialties of this region?

In the restaurant

Al ristorante [al risto'rante]

il ristorante
[il risto'rante] **restaurant**

il menù
[il me'nu] **menu**

l'antipasto
[lanti'pasto] **starter**

la portata principale
[la por'ta:ta printʃi'pa:le] **main course**

dolce
[il 'dolci] **dessert**

Ha un tavolo per due persone?   **Do you have a table for two?**
[a un 'ta:volo per 'du:e per'so:ne]

Qual è il piatto del giorno?   **What is today's special?**
['kua:l ɛ il 'pjatto del 'dʒorno]

Cosa mi consiglia?   **What would you recommend?**
['kɔ:sa mi kon'siʎʎa]

Vorrei…   **I would like…**
[vor'rɛ:i]

1. la forchetta piccola
   [la forˈketta ˈpikkola] salad fork
2. la forchetta grande
   [la forˈketta ˈgrande] dinner fork
3. il coltello grande
   [il kolˈtɛllo ˈgrande] dinner knife
4. il coltello piccolo
   [il kolˈtɛllo ˈpikkolo] salad knife
5. il cucchiaio da zuppa
   [il kukˈkja:jo da ˈtsuppa] soup spoon
6. il coltello da burro
   [il kolˈtɛllo da ˈburro] butter knife

7. la forchetta da dessert
   [la forˈketta da deˈsɛr] dessert fork
8. il cucchiaino
   [il kukkjaˈi:no] dessert spoon
9. il piattino
   [il pjatˈti:no] bread plate
10. il piatto
    [il ˈpjatto] main plate
11. il bicchiere
    [il bikˈkjɛ:re] water glass
12. il calice da vino rosso
    [il ˈka:litʃe da ˈvi:no ˈrosso] red wine glass
13. il calice da vino bianco
    [il ˈka:litʃe da ˈvi:no ˈbjanko] white wine glass

Formal table setting

La tavola apparecchiata [la 'ta:vola apparek'kja:ta]

il pepe
[il 'pe:pe]
pepper

il sale
[il 'sa:le]
salt

Seasonings

I condimenti [i kondi'menti]

il peperoncino in polvere
[il peperon'tʃi:no in 'polvere]
chili powder

il pesto
[il 'pesto]
pesto

la polvere di curry
[la 'polvere di 'kɛrri]
curry powder

la mostarda	il ketchup	la maionese
[la mos'tarda]	[il'kɛtʃap]	[la majo'ne:se]
mustard	**ketchup**	**mayonnaise**

lo zucchero	il dolcificante
[lo 'tsukkero]	[il doltʃifi'kante]
sugar	**sweetener**

la polvere di paprika	il parmigiano	la salsa di soia
[la 'polvere di 'pa:prika]	[il parmi'dʒa:no]	[la 'salsa di 'sɔ:ja]
paprika powder	**parmesan**	**soy sauce**

il pasto
[il 'pasto]

meal

la colazione
[la kolat'tsjo:ne]

breakfast

il pranzo
[il 'prandzo]

lunch

la cena
[la 'tʃe:na]

dinner

Buon appetito!

[buɔn appe'ti:to]

Enjoy your meal!

Il conto, per favore.

[il 'konto per fa'vo:re]

May I have the bill, please?

Il cibo è stato molto buono! [il 'tʃi:bo ɛ 'sta:to 'molto 'buɔ:no]	The food was very good!
Delizioso! [delit'tsjo:so]	Delicious!
Tenga il resto. ['tenga il 'rɛsto]	Keep the change.
la mancia [la 'mantʃa]	tip

la marmellata
[la marmel'la:ta]
jam

il miele
[il 'mjɛ:le]
honey

il burro d'arachidi
[il 'burro da'ra:kidi]
peanut butter

il burro
[il 'burro]
butter

il formaggio
[il for'maddʒo]
cheese

l'uovo sodo
['luɔ:vo 'sɔ:do]
soft-boiled egg

il toast
[il 'tɔst]
toast

l'omelette
[lome'lɛt]
omelet

Breakfast

La colazione [la kolat'tsjo:ne]

il muesli

[il 'mjuːzlɪ]
cereal

lo yogurt

[lo'iɔːgurt]
yogurt

la macedonia

[la matʃe'dɔːnja]
fruit salad

l'uovo al tegamino

['luɔːvo al tega'miːno]
fried egg

il prosciutto

[il proʃ'ʃutto]
ham

l'uovo strapazzato

['luɔːvo strapat'tsaːto]
scrambled eggs

PASTA

Conchiglie
[ko'ŋkiːʎe]

Penne
['penne]

Farfalle
[far'falle]

Lasagna
[la'zaːɲa]

Conchiglioni
[koŋkiʎ'ʎoːni]

Maccheroni
[makke'roːni]

Gnocchi
['ɲɔkki]

Tortellini
[tortel'liːni]

Fusilli
[fu'silli]

Ravioli
[ravi'ɔːli]

Fettuccine
[fettut'tʃiːne]

Gomiti
['goːmiti]

Pappardelle
[pappar'dɛlle]

Rigatoni
[riga'toːni]

Ruote
['ruɔːte]

Spaghetti
[spa'getti]

Tagliatelle
[taʎʎa'tɛlle]

PIZZA
['pittsa]

margherita

[marge'ri:ta]

margherita pizza

marinara

[mari'na:ra]

marinara pizza

romana

[ro'ma:na]

romana pizza

prosciutto e funghi

[proʃ'ʃutto e 'fuŋgi]

ham and mushrooms pizza

capricciosa

[kaprit'tʃo:sa]

capricciosa pizza

quattro stagioni

['kuattro sta'ʤo:ni]

four seasons pizza

quattro formaggi

['kuattro for'maddʒi]

four cheese pizza

siciliana

[sitʃi'lja:na]

Sicilian pizza

Starter

Gli antipasti [ʎi anti'pasti]

bruschetta

[brus'ketta]

bruschetta

caprese

[ka'preːse]

caprese

prosciutto e melone

[proʃ'ʃutto e me'loːne]

ham and melon

insalata di mare

[insa'laːta di 'maːre]

seafood salad

piadina

[pja'diːna]

piadina

affettato misto

[affet'taːto 'misto]

mixed cold cuts

Main course

Le portate principali [le porˈtaːte printʃiˈpaːli]

penne all'arrabbiata

[ˈpenne allarrabˈbjaːta]
penne pasta with arrabbiata sauce

risotto

[riˈsɔtto]
risotto

spaghetti alla carbonara

[spaˈgetti ˈalla karboˈnaːra]
spaghetti carbonara

spaghetti alla bolognese

[spaˈgetti alla boloɲˈɲeːse]
spaghetti bolognese

spaghetti alle vongole

[spaˈgetti alle ˈvongole]
spaghetti with clams

tagliatelle con panna e funghi

[taʎʎaˈtɛlle kon ˈpanna e ˈfuŋgi]
tagliatelle with cream and mushrooms

polenta e porcini

[poˈlɛnta e porˈtʃiːni]
polenta and porcini

Dessert

Dolci ['dolʧi]

1. il tiramisù   [il tirami'su] **tiramisu**

• • •

2. la panna cotta   [la 'panna 'kɔtta] **panna cotta**

• • •

3. la meringa   [la me'ringa] **meringue**

• • •

4. il babà   [il ba'ba] **baba**

• • •

5. il cannolo siciliano [il kan'nɔ:lo siʧi'lja:no] **Sicilian cannolo**

• • •

6. il gelato   [il dʒe'la:to] **ice-cream**

• • •

7. la torta di mele   [la 'torta di 'mɛ:le] **apple pie**

• • •

8. il bombolone   [il bombo'lo:ne] **donut**

• • •

9. il tartufo   [il tar'tu:fo] **truffle**

• • •

10. il panettone   [il panet'to:ne] **panettone**

• • •

11. il torrone   [il tor'ro:ne] **nougat**

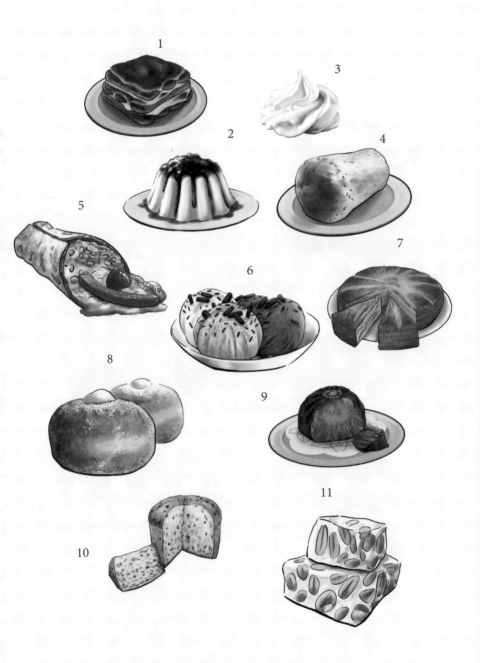

Cheeses

I formaggi [i:for'maddʒi]

Gorgonzola
[gorgon'dzɔ:la]

Mascarpone
[maskar'po:ne]

Valle d'Aosta

Lombardia

Fontina
[fon'ti:na]

Piemonte

Emillia - Ro

Liguria

Castelmagno
[kastel'maɲɲo]

Tos

Ricotta
[ri'kɔtta]

Stracchino
[strak'ki:no]

Pecorino Toscano
[peko'ri:no tos'ka:no]

Roccaccio
[rok'kattʃo]

Sardegna

Mozzarella di Bufala
[mottsa'rɛlla di 'bu:fala]

Pecorino Sardo
[peko'ri:no 'sardo]

Mozzarella
[mottsa'rɛlla]

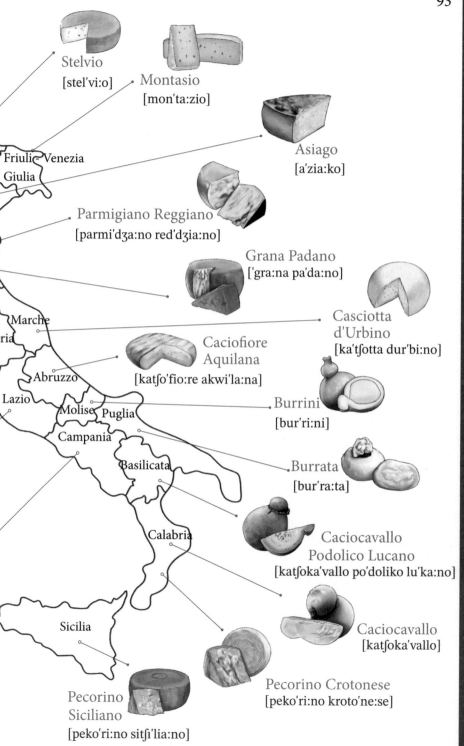

Stelvio
[stel'vi:o]

Montasio
[mon'ta:zio]

Asiago
[a'zia:ko]

Friuli Venezia
Giulia

Parmigiano Reggiano
[parmi'dʒa:no red'dʒia:no]

Grana Padano
['gra:na pa'da:no]

Casciotta
d'Urbino
[ka'tʃotta dur'bi:no]

Marche

ria

Caciofiore
Aquilana
[katʃo'fio:re akwi'la:na]

Abruzzo

Lazio

Molise Puglia

Burrini
[bur'ri:ni]

Campania

Basilicata

Burrata
[bur'ra:ta]

Calabria

Caciocavallo
Podolico Lucano
[katʃoka'vallo po'doliko lu'ka:no]

Sicilia

Caciocavallo
[katʃoka'vallo]

Pecorino Crotonese
[peko'ri:no kroto'ne:se]

Pecorino
Siciliano
[peko'ri:no sitʃi'lia:no]

Places to shop

Dove fare acquisti [ˈdoːve ˈfaːre akˈkuisti]

Alì
Auchan
Bennet
La Rinascente
Coop
Carrefour
Gigante
Oriocenter
Emisfero
Esselunga

il centro commerciale

[il 'tʃɛntro kommer'tʃaːle]
shopping center

il grande magazzino

[il 'grande magad'dziːno]
department store

il supermercato

[il supermer'kaːto]
supermarket

l'ipermercato

[lipermer'kaːto]
hypermarket

il negozio di alimentari

[il ne'gɔttsjo di alimen'taːri]
grocery store

Everything your heart desires

Tutto ciò che desideri ['tutto ʧɔ ke de'si:deri]

il negozio di cosmetici

[il ne'gɔttsjo di koz'me:titʃi]
cosmetic shop

il parrucchiere

[il parruk'kjɛ:re]
hair salon

il gioielliere

[il dʒojel'ljɛ:re]
jewellery shop

il negozio di fiori

[il ne'gɔttsjo di 'fjo:ri]
flower shop

la boutique di moda
[la buˈtik di ˈmɔːda]
fashion boutique

il negozio di calzature
[il neˈgɔttsjo di kaltsaˈtuːre]
shoe shop

il negozio di souvenir
[il neˈgɔttsjo di suveˈniːr]
souvenir shop

il negozio di antiquariato
[il neˈgɔttsjo di antikuaˈrjaːto]
antique shop

Vorrei…   I would like…
[vorˈrɛːi]

una camicia.   a shirt.
[una kaˈmiːtʃa]

un paio di pantaloni.   a pair of trousers.
[unˈpaːjo di pantaˈloːni]

un paio di scarpe.   a pair of shoes.
[unˈpaːjo di ˈskarpe]

un paio di calze.   a pair of socks.
[unˈpaːjo di ˈkaltse]

due camicette.   two blouses.
[ˈduːe kamiˈtʃette]

tre giacche.   three jackets.
[tre ˈdʒakke]

quattro gonne.   four skirts.
[ˈkuattro ˈgonne]

cinque cappotti   five coats.
[ˈtʃinkue kapˈpɔtti]

Quanto costa?
['kuanto 'kɔsta]

How much does it cost?

Costa ... euro.
['kɔsta 'ɛːuro]

It costs ... euro.

È molto costoso.
[ɛ 'molto kos'toːso]

That is very expensive.

Può farmi un prezzo migliore?
['puɔ 'faːrmi un 'prɛttso miʎ'ʎoːre]

Can you do better on price?

È molto economico.
[ɛ 'molto eko'nɔːmiko]

That is very cheap.

Grazie, va bene così.
['grattsje va 'bɛːne ko'si]

That's fine, thanks.

È a buon prezzo.
[ɛ a buɔn 'prɛttso]

The price is reasonable.

È troppo corto / troppo lungo.
[ɛ 'trɔppo 'korto / 'trɔppo 'lungo]

It's too short / too long.

È troppo stretto / troppo largo.
[ɛ 'trɔppo 'stretto / 'trɔppo 'largo]

It's too tight / too loose.

Posso provarlo?

['pɔsso pro'vaːrlo]

May I try it on?

Dov'è il camerino?

[do'vɛ il kame'riːno]

Where is the fitting room?

SALDI

['saldi]
sales

in svendita

[in 'zvendita] on sale

sconto

['skonto] discount

offerta speciale

[of'fɛrta spe'tʃa:le] special offer

promozione

[promot'tsjo:ne] promotion

Colors

I colori [i ko'lo:ri]

bianco ['bjanko]
white

nero ['nero]
black

arancio [a'rantʃo]
orange

marrone [mar'ro:ne]
brown

grigio ['gri:dʒo]
grey

blu chiaro, azzurro
[blu 'kja:ro, ad'dzurro]
light blue

chiaro
['kja:ro]
light

scuro
['sku:ro]
dark

rosso ['rosso]

red

rosa ['rɔ:za]
pink

giallo ['dʒallo]
yellow

verde ['verde]
green

blu scuro [blu 'skuro]
dark blue

viola ['vjɔ:la]
purple

Numbers

I numeri [i 'nu:meri]

0	zero	['dzɛ:ro]
1	uno	['u:no]
2	due	['du:e]
3	tre	[tre]
4	quattro	['kuattro]
5	cinque	['tʃɪnkue]
6	sei	['sɛ:i]
7	sette	['sɛtte]
8	otto	['ɔtto]
9	nove	['nɔ:ve]
10	dieci	['djɛ:tʃi]
11	undici	['unditʃi]
12	dodici	['do:ditʃi]
13	tredici	['tre:ditʃi]
14	quattordici	[kuat'torditʃi]
15	quindici	['kuinditʃi]
16	sedici	['se:ditʃi]
17	diciassette	[ditʃas'sɛtte]
18	diciotto	[di'tʃɔtto]
19	diciannove	[ditʃan'nɔ:ve]
20	venti	['venti]
21	ventuno	[ven'tu:no]
22	ventidue	[venti'du:e]
23	ventitrè	[venti'tre]
24	ventiquattro	[venti'kuattro]
25	venticinque	[venti'tʃɪŋkue]
26	ventisei	[venti'sɛ:i]
27	ventisette	[venti'sɛtte]

28	ventotto	[ven'tɔtto]
29	ventinove	[venti'nɔːve]
30	trenta	['trenta]
40	quaranta	[kua'ranta]
50	cinquanta	[tʃiŋ'kuanta]
60	sessanta	[ses'santa]
70	settanta	[set'tanta]
80	ottanta	[ot'tanta]
90	novanta	[no'vanta]
100	cento	['tʃɛnto]
101	cento uno	['tʃɛnto 'uːno]
102	cento due	['tʃɛnto 'duːe]
200	duecento	[due'tʃɛnto]
300	trecento	[tre'tʃɛnto]
400	quattrocento	[kuattro'tʃɛnto]
500	cinquecento	[tʃiŋkue'tʃɛnto]
600	seicento	[sei'tʃɛnto]
700	settecento	[sette'tʃɛnto]
800	ottocento	[otto'tʃɛnto]
900	novecento	[nove'tʃɛnto]
1000	mille	['mille]
10 000	diecimila	[djɛtʃi'miːla]
100 000	centomila	[tʃɛnto'miːla]
1 000 000	un milione	[un mi'ljoːne]

1

Primo

['pri:mo]

first

2

Secondo

[se'kondo]

second

3

Terzo

['tɛrtso]

third

fourth	quarto	['kuarto]
fifth	quinto	['kuinto]
sixth	sesto	['sɛsto]
seventh	settimo	['sɛttimo]
eighth	ottavo	[ot'ta:vo]
ninth	nono	['nɔ:no]
tenth	decimo	['dɛ:tʃimo]

When then?

Quando? ['kuando]

ieri
['jɛːri]

yesterday

ieri sera
['jɛːri 'seːra]

yesterday evening

l'altro ieri
['laltro 'jɛːri]

the day before yesterday

la settimana scorsa
[la setti'maːna 'skorsa]

last week

l'anno scorso
['lanno 'skorso]

last year

oggi

['ɔddʒi]

today

domani

[do'ma:ni]

tomorrow

dopodomani

[dopodo'ma:ni]

the day after tomorrow

la settimana prossima

[la setti'ma:na 'prɔssima]

next week

l'anno prossimo

['lanno 'prɔssimo]

next year

All about time

A proposito del tempo [a pro'pɔːzito del 'tɛmpo]

l'orario	[lo'raːrjo]	time
l'orologio	[loro'lɔːʤo]	clock
il secondo	[il se'kondo]	second
dei secondi	['deːi se'kondi]	seconds
il minuto	[il mi'nuːto]	minute
dei minuti	['deːi mi'nuːti]	minutes
il quarto d'ora	[il 'kuarto 'doːra]	quarter of an hour
la mezz'ora	[mɛd'dzoːra]	half an hour
l'ora	['loːra]	hour
delle ore	['delle 'oːre]	hours

il mattino

[il mat'ti:no]

morning

il mezzogiorno

[il meddzo'dʒorno]

noon

il pomeriggio

[il pome'riddʒo]

afternoon

la sera

[la 'se:ra]

evening

la notte

[la 'nɔtte]

night

la mezzanotte

[la meddza'nɔtte]

midnight

presto
['prɛsto]
early

tardi
['tardi]
late

Che ore sono?

[ke 'oːre 'soːno]

What time is it?

7:10
Sono le sette e dieci.
['soːno le 'sɛtte e 'djɛːtʃi]
It's ten past seven a.m.

E' l'una.

[ɛ 'luːna]

It's one a.m.

7:15
Sono le sette e un quarto.

['soːno le 'sɛtte e un 'kuarto]
It's a quarter past seven a.m.

7: 55
Sono le otto meno cinque.

['soːno le 'ɔtto 'meːno 'tʃinkue]
It's five to eight a.m.

08:00

Sono le otto di mattina.

['so:no le 'ɔtto di mat'ti:na]

It's eight a.m.

9:50

Sono le dieci meno dieci.

['so:no le 'djɛ:tʃi 'me:no 'djɛ:tʃi]

It's ten to ten a.m.

10:00

Sono le dieci in punto.

['so:no le 'djɛ:tʃi in 'punto]

It's ten a.m.

10:10

Sono le dieci e dieci.

['so:no le 'djɛ:tʃi e 'djɛ:tʃi]

It's ten past ten a.m.

10:30

Sono le dieci e mezza.

['so:no le 'djɛ:tʃɪ e 'mɛddza]

It's half past ten a.m.

12:00

Sono le dodici. / È mezzogiorno.

['so:no le 'do:ditʃɪ / ɛ meddzo'dʒo:rno]

It's midday.

17:45

Sono le sei meno un quarto di sera.

['so:no le 'sɛ:i 'me:no un'kuarto di 'se:ra]

It's a quater to six p.m.

20:00

Sono le otto di sera.

['so:no le 'ɔtto di 'se:ra]

It's eight p.m.

Seven days of the week

I giorni della settimana
[i 'dʒorni 'della setti'ma:na]

domenica	**lunedì**	**martedì**
[do'me:nika]	[lune'di]	[marte'di]
Sunday	Monday	Tuesday

il giorno lavorativo   work day
[il 'dʒorno lavora'ti:vo]

il fine settimana   weekend
[il 'fi:ne setti'ma:na]

il giorno festivo   vacation
[il 'dʒorno fes'ti:vo]

il giorno di riposo   rest day
[il 'dʒorno di ri'pɔ:so]

mercoledì	**giovedì**	**venerdì**	**sabato**
[merkole'di]	[dʒove'di]	[vener'di]	['sa:bato]
Wednesday	Thursday	Friday	Saturday

Che giorno è oggi?
[ke 'dʒorno ɛ 'ɔddʒi]

What day is it today?

Oggi è lunedì.
['ɔddʒi ɛ lune'di]

It's Monday.

Quanti ne abbiamo oggi?
['kuanti ne ab'bia:mo 'ɔddʒi]

What date is it today?

Oggi è il 10 di gennaio.
['ɔddʒi ɛ il 'djɛ:tʃi di dʒen'na:jo]

It's the 10th of January.

Oggi è un giorno festivo?
['ɔddʒi ɛ un 'dʒorno fes'ti:vo]

Is today a holiday?

1
gennaio
[dʒenˈnaːjo]
January

2
febbraio
[febˈbraːjo]
February

5
maggio
[ˈmaddʒo]
May

6
giugno
[ˈdʒuɲɲo]
June

9
settembre
[setˈtɛmbre]
September

10
ottobre
[otˈtoːbre]
October

The twelve months of the year

I dodici mesi dell'anno [i 'do:ditʃɪ 'me:si dɛl'lanno]

3

marzo

['martso]

March

4

aprile

[a'pri:le]
April

7

luglio

['luʎʎo]
July

8

agosto

[a'gosto]
August

11

novembre

[no'vɛmbre]
November

12

dicembre

[di'tʃɛmbre]
December

The weather and seasons

Il clima e le stagioni [il ˈkliːma e le staˈdʒoːni]

la primavera

[la primaˈvɛːra]

spring

l'estate

[lesˈtaːte]

summer

l'autunno

[lauˈtunno]

fall

l'inverno

[linˈvɛrno]

winter

Che tempo fa oggi? What's the weather like today?
[ke 'tɛmpo fa 'ɔddʒi]

Oggi il tempo è bello. The weather is fine today.
['ɔddʒi il 'tɛmpo ɛ 'bɛllo]

C'è il sole. It's sunny.
[tʃe il 'so:le]

Oggi il tempo è brutto. The weather is bad today.
['ɔddʒi il 'tɛmpo ɛ 'brutto]

Fa caldo. It's hot.
[fa 'kaldo]

Fa molto caldo. It's very hot.
[fa 'molto 'kaldo]

Ho molto caldo. I'm boiling.
[ɔ 'molto 'kaldo]

Fa molto freddo. It's really cold.
[fa 'molto 'freddo]

Ho molto freddo. I'm freezing.
[ɔ 'molto 'freddo].

C'è vento. It's windy.
[tʃe 'vɛnto]

C'è nebbia. It's foggy.
[tʃe 'nebbja]

Piove. It's rainy.
['pjɔ:ve]

Pioviggina. It's drizzling.
[pjo'viddʒina]

Nevica. It's snowing.
['ne:vika]

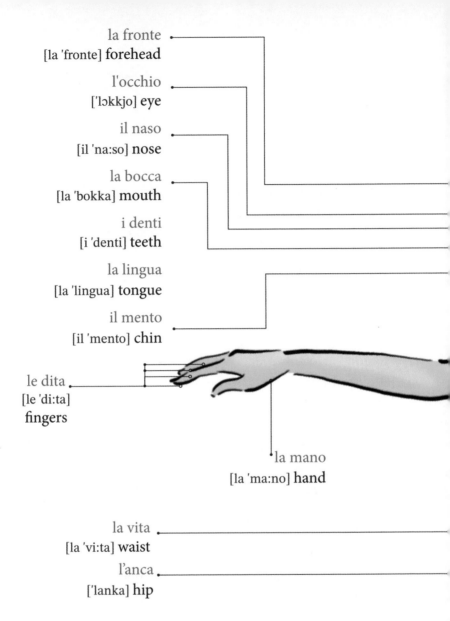

la fronte
[la 'fronte] **forehead**

l'occhio
['lɔkkjo] **eye**

il naso
[il 'na:so] **nose**

la bocca
[la 'bokka] **mouth**

i denti
[i 'denti] **teeth**

la lingua
[la 'lingua] **tongue**

il mento
[il 'mento] **chin**

le dita
[le 'di:ta]
fingers

la mano
[la 'ma:no] **hand**

la vita
[la 'vi:ta] **waist**

l'anca
['lanka] **hip**

Parts of the body

Le parti del corpo [le 'parti del 'kɔrpo]

la testa
[la 'tɛsta] head

il viso
[il 'vi:zo] face

l'orecchio
[lo'rekkjo] ear

la guancia
[la 'gwantʃa] cheek

il collo
[il 'kollo] neck

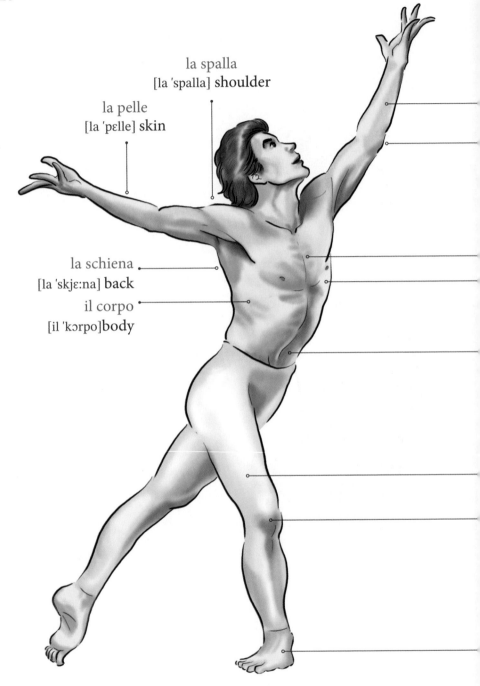

la spalla
[la 'spalla] shoulder

la pelle
[la 'pɛlle] skin

la schiena
[la 'skjɛːna] back

il corpo
[il 'kɔrpo]body

il braccio
[il 'brattʃo] arm

il gomito
[il 'goːmito] elbow

il petto
[il 'pɛtto] chest

il cuore
[il 'kuɔːre] heart

la pancia
[la 'pantʃa] stomach

la gamba
[la 'gamba] leg

il ginocchio
[il dʒi'nɔkkjo] knee

il piede
[il 'pjɛːde] foot

When you feel sick

Quando ci si sente male ['kuando ʧi si 'sente 'ma:le]

Sono malato. ['so:no ma'la:to]	I don't feel well.
Mi viene da vomitare. [mi 'vje:ne da vomi'tar: e]	I need to vomit.
Ho nausea. [ɔ 'na:uzea]	I feel nauseous.
Fa male qui. [fa 'ma:le ku'i]	It hurts here.
Ho la febbre. [ɔ la 'fɛbbre]	I have a fever.
Ho mal di testa. [ɔ mal di 'tɛsta]	I have a headache.
Ho mal di pancia. [ɔ mal di 'pantʃa]	I have a stomachache.

Ho mal di gola. [ɔ mal di 'goːla]	I have a sore throat.
Ho mal di schiena. [ɔ mal di 'skjɛːna]	I have backache.
Ho mal di denti. [ɔ mal di 'denti]	I have a toothache.
Soffro di stitichezza. ['sɔffro di stiti'kettsa]	I am constipated.
Ho la diarrea. [ɔ la diar'rɛːa]	I have diarrhoea.
Ho un'allergia. [ɔ unaller'dʒiːa]	I have an allergy.
Ho prurito. [ɔ pru'riːto]	I'm itchy.

La farmacia

[la farma'tʃiːa] pharmacy

l'ospedale

[lospe'daːle] hospital

la medicina

[la medi'tʃiːna] medicine

il medico / il dottore

[il 'mɛːdiko / il dot'toːre] doctor

l'infermiere

[linfer'mjeːre] (male) nurse

l'infermiera

[linfer'mjeːra] (female) nurse

Salute!

[sa'luːte]

Bless you!

Urgency

Emergenze [[emer'dʒɛntse]

Ho urgentemente bisogno di un bagno.

[ɔ urdʒɛnte'mente bi'zoːɲo di un 'baːɲo]

I need to go to the toilet.

Dov'è il bagno?

[do'vɛ il 'baːɲo]

Where is the toilet?

C'è un bagno pubblico qui?

['tʃɛ un 'baːɲo 'pubbliko ku'i]

Is there a public toilet near here?

Devo andare immediatamente all'ospedale.

['dɛːvo an'daːre immedjata'mente allospe'daːle]

I need to go to the hospital.

Chiamate la polizia, per favore!

[kja'ma:te la polit'tsi:a per fa'vo:re]

Call the police, please!

What do these signs mean?

Cosa ci dicono i segnali? [ˈkɔːsa tʃi ˈdiːkono i seˈɲaːli]

ATTENZIONE

[attenˈtsjoːne]

WARNING

SENSO VIETATO

[ˈsɛnso vjeˈtaːto]

NO ENTRY

DIVIETO D'ACCESSO

[diˈvjɛːto datˈtʃɛsso]

RESTRICTED AREA

PERICOLO DI MORTE

[peˈriːkolo di ˈmɔrte]

DANGER OF DEATH

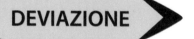

DEVIAZIONE

[deviatˈtsjoːne]

DETOUR

ATTENZIONE, SCUOLA!

[attenˈtsjoːne ˈskuɔːla]

ATTENTION, SCHOOL

PARCHEGGIO

[par'keddʒo]

PARKING

SENSO UNICO

['sɛnso 'u:niko]

ONE WAY

DIVIETO DI PARCHEGGIO

[di'vjɛ:to di par'keddʒo]

NO PARKING

PASSO CARRABILE
LASCIARE LIBERO IL PASSAGGIO

['passo kar'ra:bile laʃ'ʃa:re 'li:bero il pas'saddʒo]

PLEASE DO NOT PARK
VEHICLES EXIT

INGRESSO RISERVATO
AL PERSONALE

[in'grɛsso riser'va:to al perso'na:le]

NOTICE AUTHORIZED
STAFF ONLY

RISERVATO AI RESIDENTI

[riser'va:to 'a:i resi'dɛ:nti]

RESERVED PARKING
FOR RESIDENTS ONLY

SPINGERE

['spindʒere]

PUSH

TIRARE

[ti'ra:re]

PULL

NON DISTURBARE

[non distur'ba:re]

PLEASE DO NOT DISTURB

VIETATO L'ACCESSO AL
PERSONALE NON AUTORIZZATO

[vje'ta:to lat'tʃɛsso al perso'na:le

non autorid'dza:to]

AUTHORIZED STAFF ONLY

TOILETTE DONNE

[tua'lɛt 'dɔnne]

WOMEN TOILET

TOILETTE UOMINI

[tua'lɛt 'uɔ:mini]

MEN TOILET

APERTO

[a'pɛrto]

OPEN

CHIUSO

['kju:so]

CLOSE

PASSAGGIO PEDONALE

[pas'saddʒo pedo'na:le]

PEDESTRIAN CROSSING

RISERVATO

[riser'va:to]

RESERVED

PRONTO SOCCORSO

['pronto sok'korso]

FIRST AID

USCITA D'EMERGENZA

[uʃ'ʃi:ta demer'dʒɛntsa]

EMERGENCY EXIT

Emotional outbursts

In this chapter we will be dealing with something rather special: emotional outbursts. What, you may ask, does this have to do with a book aimed at introducing a foreign language?

I know that this is quite a sensitive issue and I'm pretty sure that you don't know any other language books that deal with the topic. As I say, I'm inviting you on a risky adventure. But I think it's absolutely essential for you and really useful. I think you need to know this because it can help you to avoid very embarrassing situations when you are in Italy.

First, let me explain what I mean by emotional outbursts. What exactly are they? They are words that simply tumble out of your mouth. You don't usually give them a second thought – they just pop out – and can't be popped back in again, once they're out.

When we are angry, disappointed, afraid, surprised or delighted, we use emotional outbursts to let off steam and regain our calm. We can think of them as turbulence tranquilizers for our emotions.

These outbursts can be more or less violent, depending on intonation and the particular intention or situation in which they are spoken. Gentle outbursts can be mumbled to ourselves to cool our spirits. Violent emotional outbursts are often insulting and deeply hurtful. This type is known in Italian as Parolaccia.

So, you can probably now appreciate how difficult and tricky this whole topic is. These words and phrases are used unconsciously all the time all over the world. The fact that I bring up this topic may be unpleasant for the Italian who are often reserved and polite by nature. However, my intentions are entirely good. I don't want to insult or ridicule their language, but simply to help you avoid making a fool of yourself.

If you hear these Italian words and try to copy them, it's more than likely that you'll get the exact intonation wrong, or it won't come out at quite the right moment, or be appropriate for the person or situation you're in.

So, my first tip is: don't block your ears when you hear them, but don't just copy them either. As a foreigner, you need to get to know them but use them carefully, and only if you're absolutely certain about how and when.

But even if you never use these outbursts yourself, it is certainly helpful to know them. It might avoid a few embarrassing situations or even a slap around the face. This is one of the main reasons for dealing with these phrases.

I hope I've been able to make clear why this topic is an important one in language learning.

Let's turn to a very common expression in Italian: "Mamma mia!". You will hear this everywhere you go in Italy. It's used both by young and old, and by men as well as women. The term is as much a part of the Italian way of life as pasta. You will come across both on a daily basis.

Italians use this outburst to express both delight and surprise or shock. Imagine two young Italian men out for a stroll in the town. A beautiful young girl comes around the corner. Their first reaction: "Mamma mia!". The literal translation is "my mother".

Now it's true that most Italians love their mothers at least as much as their pasta, but in the case of the two Italian youngsters, their thoughts are probably completely taken up by this new beautiful girl.

The second expression we will consider is the word "Merda!". This word literally means the organic waste matter from the digestive system. There is a corresponding word in English but it would be bad manners to print it here. Everyone knows the expression, and there are corresponding words in every language so I do not need to add anything.

Next, we will turn to the outburst "Cavolo!".

"Cavolo" is used as a mild insult, but it is not a strong swear word. In fact it can be used jokingly as well as seriously. The literal translation is "cabbage" and is used to describe someone who is not intellegent.

The next term "Che diamine!" is a expression that refers to a very unpleasant place, namely hell. However, it does count as a very strong swear word in Italian. It corresponds more or less to the English expression "What the hell!", which clearly expresses anger but is still quite respectable and is common in all levels of society.

You will also hear the word "Stupido!" which is an exact translation of "stupid". I don't think I need to add much by way of explanation. Referring to the limits of someone's intellegence is a common way of insulting someone all over the world. Perhaps I should add that if the person in question is female, the Italians will use the feminine form: "Stupida!".

A slightly stronger version of the same idea is the word "Idiota!" We all know what being called an idiot means, so I don't need to add much. In this case Italians will use the same word whether they are referring to a man or a woman.

Now let's turn to stronger expressions that aim clearly below the belt. Most decent Italians might be horrified to read the following words, and could consider a reference to them as an insult to their language. As I have already said, this is not my intention in writing this book. In order to respect their feelings, I have decided to use a kind of code. I will not write the word itself but use a phonetic alphabet table. This also has the useful side effect that you will learn how to spell the words.

The first word in this category can be coded as follows: Savona, Torino, Roma, Otranto, Napoli, Zara, Otranto . This is a very rude outburst which compares the person in question to the lower end of our digestive system.

Unfortunately , I don't think there are many languages in the world who can boast that they do not have a similar expression in their own language. The feminine version is: Savona, Torino, Roma, Otranto, Napoli, Zara, Ancona.

The following expression is an outburst made up of three words. It's a swear word that describes the son of a lady, whose profession involves a lot of lying down. In fact, the speaker is not referring to a particular profession nor is he interested in any family relationships. What the term really expresses is an extremely rude way of insulting someone. Here are the words in coded form:

Firenze, Imola, Genova, Livorno, Imola, Otranto
Domodossola, Imola
Padova, Udine, Torino, Torino, Ancona, Napoli, Ancona

"Fi......!"

This is a topic that is extremely sensitive and can be upsetting, especially when we are dealing with very strong swear words. When we really want to hurt someone, we often use terms referring to the sexes. This is actually rather strange, since sexuality should be something we are attracted to in a positive way. Why this should be the case, I cannot explain.

This kind of outburst is very common and is used on a daily basis in Italy. And let's face it, it is something that is common to all languages. The outburst in question is:

Como, Ancona, Zara, Zara, Otranto.

Literally it is a vulgar reference to the male genitalia, but this is not what is on the speaker's mind at all. What he really wants to express is disgust towards the person he is referring to. This is something most of us know from our own languages.

Let's stay in this area of the human anatomy, even if it does make us blush! The next expression is made up of three words:

Torino, Empoli, Savona, Torino, Ancona
Domodossola, Imola
Como, Ancona, Zara, Zara, Otranto.

I have already discussed the meaning of the last word. "Di" means "of" and "testa" means "head". I will leave the full meaning of this expression to your imagination. The intention of this outburst is clearly to insult and hurt the person in question.

Let me repeat the reasoning behind this description of emotional outbursts. I do not intend to train you to become experts in the use of Italian swear words. On the contrary, I want to protect you from the darkest excesses of vulgarity.

The last two expressions both mean the same thing. One is simply a shorter version of the other. A literal translation will take us to the backside – to the exit of our digestive system.

The first expression in coded form is:

Firenze, Ancona, Napoli, Como, Udine, Livorno, Otranto.

The second is:

Venezia, Ancona, Firenze, Firenze, Ancona, Napoli, Como, Udine, Livorno, Otranto.

I will not go into any further detail. I think it is enough to say that the speaker here is expressing his disgust and contempt for the person in question and is deadly serious about it.

Finally, dear readers, let me assure you that I have tried to do all I can to deal with such a sensitive and controversial issue without embarrassing you. I strongly believe that it is important to give you as much confidence as possible when starting to learn the Italian language.

Knowing something about how people express their feelings and emotions is part of that process. I could continue on this theme for some time, but it's enough for you to have a clear idea of the topic, so that you can avoid any embarrassing situations.

Never forget that emotional outburst can vary in meaning as well as in intensity. If you hear one of these phrases, see if you can hear whether the speaker is angry, dissatisfied, furious, or perhaps cracking a joke or making fun of someone.

As far as possible, avoid using these outbursts yourself. Remember, that these words have the power to insult and hurt others and can also be dangerous for you. By using them you are likely to put yourself in a very embarrassing situation, and quite possibly lose face in the process.

Bravo!
['braːvo] Bravo!

Grandioso!
[gran'djoːso] Great!

Ottimo!
['ɔttimo] Excellent!

Perfetto!
[per'fɛtto] Perfect!

Compliments

Complimenti [kompli'menti]

Magnifico!
[ma'ɲiːfiko]

Magnificient!

Meraviglioso!
[meraviʎ'ʎoːso]

Marvelous!

Romance

Frasi romantiche ['fra:zi ro'mantike]

Sei così bello.
['sɛːi ko'si 'bɛllo]
You are so handsome.

───

Hai degli occhi bellissimi.
['aːi 'deʎʎi 'ɔkkj be'lissimi]
You have got beautiful eyes.

───

Sei unico / straordinario.
['sɛːi 'uːniko / straordi'naːrjo]
You are unique.

───

Ti voglio bene.
[ti voʎ'ʎo 'bɛːne]
I like you very much.

───

Ti amo.
[ti 'aːmo]
I love you.

───

Ti amo tanto.
[ti 'aːmo 'tanto]
I love you very much.

Sei così bella.

[ˈsɛːi koˈsi ˈbɛlla]

You are so beautiful.

Sei meravigliosa.

['sɛːi meraviʎˈʎosa]

You are splendid.

Ti amo.
[ti 'a:mo]

I love you.

Vorresti sposarmi?

[vor'rɛsti spo'zarmi]

Will you marry me?

Ti amo tanto.

[ti 'a:mo 'tanto]

I love you so much.

Land and people

Il paese e il popolo [il pa'eːze e il 'pɔːpolo]

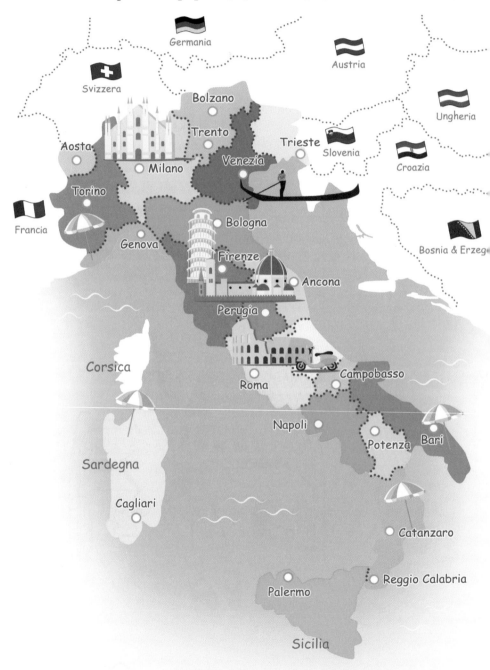

If you want to learn about the shape and form of Italy, the simplest thing to do is to look at a map. If you want to know more about the people, how they think, how they lead their lives, then the best method is to look at their proverbs. They reveal how the Italian "tick".

Often proverbs have developed over centuries as the result of local people's experiences and of the way they think and live their lives. These sayings are passed on from one generation to the next, together with the emotions and moods they convey. Here are a few memorable Italian proverbs:

Tra il dire e il fare c'è di mezzo il mare.
[tra il 'diːre e il 'faːre tʃɛ di 'mɛddzo il 'maːre]
Between saying and doing there is a sea.

Chi dorme non piglia pesci.
[ki 'dorme non 'piʎʎa 'peʃʃi]
He who sleeps does not catch fish.

Gente allegra, Dio l'aiuta.
['dʒɛnte al'leːgra 'diːo la'juːta]
Cheerful people, God help them.

Patti chiari, amici cari.
['patti 'kjaːri a'miːtʃi 'kaːri]
Clear deals, dear friends.

Amore regge senza legge.
[a'moːre 'rɛddʒe 'sɛntsa 'leddʒe]
Love rules without law.

Now you will be able to savor the Italian language like a delicatessen. Any worries you may have had about learning this language will turn to joyful confidence.

Italian
at your Fingertips

by
Tien Tammada

Original title: อิตาลีทันใจพูดได้ด้วยปลายนิ้ว เทียร ธรรมดา
© Leelaaphasa.Co.,Ltd.
63/120 Moo 8, Tambon Saothonghin, Bangyai District,
Nonthaburi 11140 Thailand
E-Mail: leelaaphasa2008@gmail.com
All rights reserved.

1. Edition 2024 (1,01 - 2024)
© PONS Langenscheidt GmbH, Stöckachstraße 11, 70190 Stuttgart, 2024

Translation: Ta Tammadien, Hubert Möller, David Thron
Correction: Vanda Liber, Kidan Patanant, Ursula Eriberti,
Francesco J. Cucinotta
Cover Design: Leonie Eul
Illustrations Inside: K. Kiattisak, Netitorn Terdbankird
Photo Credit Cover: lenaalyonushka/Shutterstock, ambassador806S/Getty
Images
Typesetting/Layout: Wachana Leuwattananon, Vipoo Lerttasanawanish
Printing and Binding: Multiprint GmbH, Konstinbrod

ISBN 978-3-12-514624-2